Guess What!

Activity Book 6

with Online Resources

British English

Susan Rivers

Series Editor: Lesley Koustaff

CAMBRIDGE
UNIVERSITY PRESS

CAMBRIDGE
UNIVERSITY PRESS

University Printing House, Cambridge CB2 8BS, United Kingdom

One Liberty Plaza, 20th Floor, New York, NY 10006, USA

477 Williamstown Road, Port Melbourne, VIC 3207, Australia

314–321, 3rd Floor, Plot 3, Splendor Forum, Jasola District Centre, New Delhi – 110025, India

79 Anson Road, #06–04/06, Singapore 079906

Cambridge University Press is part of the University of Cambridge.

It furthers the University's mission by disseminating knowledge in the pursuit of education, learning and research at the highest international levels of excellence.

www.cambridge.org
Information on this title: www.cambridge.org/9781107545557

First published 2016

20 19 18 17 16 15 14 13 12 11

Printed in Malaysia by Vivar Printing

A catalogue record for this publication is available from the British Library

ISBN 978-1-107-54555-7 Activity Book with Online Resources Level 6
ISBN 978-1-107-54550-2 Pupil's Book Level 6
ISBN 978-1-107-12314-4 Teacher's Book with DVD Level 6
ISBN 978-1-107-54557-1 Class Audio CDs Level 6
ISBN 978-1-107-54559-5 Presentation Plus DVD-ROM Level 6
ISBN 978-1-107-54570-0 Teacher's Resource and Tests CD-ROM Levels 5–6

Additional resources for this publication at www.cambridge.org/guesswhat

Contents

Seasons and weather

1 **Read and complete the sentences.**

1 It rains every day in ___monsoon___ season.

2 There isn't any rain in a _____ .

3 _____ is colder than autumn.

4 A lot of plants and flowers start to grow in _____ .

5 We can often see lightning and hear _____ in a _____ .

2 (Think) **Circle the odd one out.**

1 summer (storm) autumn
2 winter flood drought
3 thunder monsoon lightning

3 **Read and write the words. Then number the pictures.**

1 This is the hottest season. ___summer___

2 This is the coldest season. _____

3 This is when it rains too much and there's water in the streets and buildings. _____

4 Leaves change colour and fall from the trees in this season. _____

5 This is the light we see in the sky in a storm. _____

6 This is when it doesn't rain for a long time and the land is very dry. _____

My picture dictionary → Go to page 84: Write the new words.

4 **Read and circle the correct words.**

1 There _____ rain, but there _____ any thunder or lightning.

   a (was, wasn't)   **b** did, didn't

2 _____ they play football in the rain? Yes, they _____ .

   a Were, were   **b** Did, did

3 Pablo _____ go windsurfing because it _____ windy.

   a wasn't, didn't   **b** didn't, wasn't

4 _____ your holiday fun? No, it _____ .

   a Was, wasn't   **b** Did, didn't

5 Maria _____ enjoy her holiday because there _____ a lot of storms.

   a weren't, did   **b** didn't, were

5 **Complete the questions and answers.**

Anna and Claire's summer holiday

1 Where ____*did*____ Anna go in the summer holidays? She _____ to Bali with her cousin, Claire.

2 What _____ the weather like? It _____ hot and sunny.

3 What _____ they do? They _____ to the beach every day.

4 _____ there sharks in the sea? No, there _____ , but there _____ dolphins.

6 **Look at activity 5. Write questions.**

1 *Did Anna go to Bali in the spring holidays?*
No, she didn't. She went in the summer holidays.

2 _____
No, it wasn't. It was hot and sunny.

3 _____
Yes, they did. They went every day.

4 _____
Yes, there were. There were a lot of dolphins.

5 _____
Yes, it was. It was a lot of fun!

7 **Join the two sentences using *when*.**

1 The students were excited. They visited the museum.

The students were excited when
they visited the museum.

2 Gemma's grandmother moved house. She felt sad.

_____

_____

3 The weather was awful. Luke and Kate arrived.

_____

4 Peter saw the bat. He was scared.

_____

5 My father went to India. He lost his mobile phone.

_____

8 **Put the words in order.**

1 was / storm / yesterday. / There / a

There was a storm yesterday.

2 saw / happy / Lisa / when / was / her cousins. / she

_____

3 rock climbing / didn't / Karen / go / last week.

_____

4 Juan / ten, / was / When / went / he / to Brazil.

_____

5 floods / were / There / my town / last month. / in

_____

9 **My World Complete the sentences about you.**

1 When I was five, _____ .

2 I felt happy when _____ .

3 When _____ , I felt sad.

10 **Think** Read the story again. Circle the correct words and then number.

a Jack and Ruby are **surprised/happy** to help Sofia with the island game.

b Ruby wants to go back to the house because there's a **storm/flood**.

c She wants to **enter/watch** a computer game competition.

1 d Jack is surprised to see (Sofia)/Ruby.

11 Read and match the questions and answers.

1 Who is Jack surprised to see? | c | a Yes, they do.

2 What does Sofia want to enter?   b No, it isn't.

3 Do Jack and Ruby want to help her?   c Sofia.

4 Is the game finished?   d Because there's a dangerous storm.

5 Why is Ruby scared?   e A computer game competition.

12 **My World** What can you do to show the value: ask your friends for help?

1 *You can ask a friend for help with your homework.*

2 _____

3 _____

Skills: *Reading*

13 Read Tom's article in the Pineville school newsletter.
Complete with the past tense of the words in the box.

~~is~~   isn't   are   rain   go   help   start   arrive   stay   see

Bad storm hits Pineville!
By Tom Banks

There ¹___*was*___ a dangerous storm in Pineville last Sunday
night. It ²_____ at 9.00 p.m. At first, it was very windy
and there was a lot of thunder and lightning. Then it
⁴_____ for a long time. There ³_____
floods at the Pineville Shopping Centre and the bus station. A lot of
trees fell down. The police ⁵_____ people get home.
It was very scary.

When the teachers, Mr Jones and Ms Green, ⁶_____
at our school on Monday morning, they were surprised. They
⁷_____ water in our dining hall, and there was a big
tree in the library! The teachers had to leave the school because it
⁸_____ safe. The Pineville pupils ⁹_____
at home last Monday, but they ¹⁰_____ back to school
last Tuesday. The library is closed until next week. What a mess!

14 Read and write *true* or *false*.

1   The storm started at 8.00 p.m. last Sunday night.   ___*false*___

2   There was thunder, lighting and a lot of wind.   _____

3   The Pineville Shopping Centre fell down.   _____

4   There was a flood in the bus station.   _____

5   The teachers had to stay in the school.   _____

6   The Pineville pupils didn't go to school on Monday.   _____

15   **TIP**   **A noun is a word that names a person, place or thing.**
Tom Banks lives in *Pineville*.
There was a *storm*.
Read Tom's article again. Circle six examples of nouns.

Skills: *Writing*

16 **Make notes about a weather event in your town.**

Weather event:	
Where:	
When:	
What happened:	1
	2
	3
	4
	5

17 **Write an article about a weather event in your town.**

Title:

What do the shadows in the painting tell us?

1 **Read and match.**

1	We see short shadows	d	a	when the sun is on the right.
2	Shadows are long		b	when the light comes from the side.
3	Artists paint shadows on the right		c	when the sun is on the left.
4	The shadows are on the left		d	when the light comes from above.
5	In winter paintings, we often		e	see long shadows.

2 **Circle the shadow in the two drawings. Then answer the questions.**

1   Where is the shadow in each picture?

In picture a, it's on the right of the tree.

2   Where is the sun in each picture?

3   Is the shadow in each picture long or short?

4   What season is it in each picture?

3 **In your notebook, draw and write about the things you can see outside and their shadows.**

Evaluation

1 **Look at Lisa's diary. Then read and circle the correct words.**

Lisa's spring diary

Sunday	Monday	Tuesday	Wednesday	Thursday	Friday	Saturday
Snowy	Sunny and cold *Spring holiday	Cloudy and warmer	Thunder and lightning storms *Arrived in Florida!	Rain and wind	Rain and wind	Flood! *Left Florida!

This is Lisa's ¹**spring**/summer diary. It ²**was**/**were** cold on Sunday and Monday. Lisa and her family ³**were**/**went** to Florida on Wednesday. When they arrived, there was an awful ⁴**drought**/**storm**. They had to leave Florida because there was a ⁵**flood**/**rain**.

2 **Look at activity 1. Answer the questions.**

1 What was the weather like on Monday?

It was sunny and cold on Monday.

2 Did Lisa visit Florida in winter?

_____

3 What was the weather like when they arrived in Florida?

_____

4 What was the weather like on Thursday?

_____

5 Was there a drought in Florida?

_____

6 Did Lisa enjoy her holiday?

_____

3 **Complete the sentences about this unit.**

✓ = I can …   ✗ = I can't …

☐ 1 … name four seasons.

☐ 2 … talk about dangerous weather.

☐ 3 … talk and ask about things that happened in the past.

☐ 4 … talk about two things that happened at the same time using *when*.

☐ 5 … talk about asking a friend for help.

6 The part of this unit I found the most interesting was _____ .

1 **Read and write *true* or *false*.**

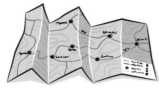

1 A rucksack helps us see at night.   *false*

2 We can keep warm with a blanket.   _____

3 People usually drink coffee from a bowl.   _____

4 We can sleep in a sleeping bag when we haven't got a bed.   _____

5 People usually eat pizza from a cup.   _____

2 **Think** **Read and write the words.**

sleeping bag   bowl   rucksack   torch   water bottle   plate   tent   cup

1 Things we can open and close.

   sleeping bag _____

2 Things we use for eating and drinking.

   _____   _____   _____

3 Things we usually use at night.

   _____   _____   _____

3 **My World** **Which camping things have you got? Complete the sentences.**

1 I've got _____ .

2 I haven't got _____ .

My picture dictionary ➡ Go to page 85: Write the new words.

4 **Read and complete the sentences. Use the words in brackets.**

1 Sam _____wanted to go_____ camping with his class last month. (want / go)

2 He _____ early that morning, but he forgot to set his alarm clock. (need / get up)

3 Then he forgot his sleeping bag, so he _____ home and get it. (have / run)

4 He _____ very fast to the bus stop, but he was too late. (try / run)

5 His mum _____ him to the campsite. (have / drive)

5 **Put the words in order.**

1 go / Maria / to / mountain biking. / and / wanted / her family
   Maria and her family wanted to go mountain biking.

2 the / take / camping trip. / a sleeping bag / forgot / My brother / to / on
   _____

3 this / bed / I / to / my / had / make / morning.
   _____

4 their / do / needed / The students / to / homework / last night.
   _____

5 was / started / The baby / tired. / because / to / she / cry
   _____

6 **My World** **Complete the sentences about you. Use the words in the box.**

| want   need   have |

1 I _____ yesterday.

2 I _____ last night.

3 I _____ this morning.

7 Look at the table. Then answer the questions.

Ms Lee's Year 6 Class *To do* list

sweep the floor	water the plants	collect the books	tidy the classroom	wash the cups	turn off the computers
Diego Anna	Sam Ellie	Ben Joe	Hae Akoi	Harry Olivia	Elena Leila

1 What did Ms Lee ask Ben to do?

 She asked him to collect the books.

2 What did she ask Elena to do?

 _____

3 What did she ask Sam and Ellie to do?

 _____

4 What did she ask Harry to do?

 _____

5 What did she ask Anna to do?

 _____

8 Look at activity 7. Write the questions.

1 *What did Ms Lee ask Olivia to do?*

 She asked her to wash the cups.

2 _____

 She asked them to tidy the classroom.

3 _____

 She asked him to sweep the floor.

4 _____

 She asked them to collect the books.

5 _____

 She asked her to water the plants.

9 (Think) **Read the story again. Correct the mistakes and then number.**

[ ] **a** The children make tents with sleeping bags and camp in the forest. _____

[ ] **b** The naughty ants are trying to show them something. _____

[1] **c** Ruby, Jack and Sofia are on an island in Sofia's ~~book~~. _____*game*_____

[ ] **d** They find a photo of the island. _____

10 **Read and circle the correct answers.**

1 Where are the children?
  a They're at home.   **b** (They're on an island.)

2 What are the ants doing?
  a They're showing the children a map.   **b** They're showing the children the island.

3 Where is the map?
  a It's in a tree.   **b** It's in a tent.

4 Have the children got tents in their rucksacks?
  a Yes, they have.   **b** No, they haven't.

5 What do they use to make tents?
  a They use blankets.   **b** They use maps.

11 (My World) **What can you do to show the value: be resourceful?**

1 *You can use a stick to get something out of water.*

2 You can use the internet to _____

_____

3 You can use _____

to _____

Story   Value   **15**

Skills: *Reading*

12 **Read and complete the story. Use the words in brackets.**

Carol is a clever girl, but she always forgets things. One day, she went hiking in the jungle. It [1] _started_ (start) to rain. She [2] _____ (forget) to [3] _____ (take) an umbrella, so she [4] _____ (have) to use a big leaf to keep dry. Then she got very thirsty. She forgot [5] _____ (take) her water bottle, so she [6] _____ (have) to [7] _____ (use) her hat to get water from a waterfall. She was tired. She [8] _____ (forget) to take a sleeping bag, so she [9] _____ (need) to [10] _____ (put) her blanket between two trees. She tried [11] _____ (go) home, but she [12] _____ (get) lost because she didn't have a map. She [13] _____ (need) to go west, so she [14] _____ (look) at the sun to find her way home. Carol is a very clever girl!

13 **Look at activity 12. Read and complete the sentences.**

> Carol forgot to take _an umbrella_ . → She used _a big leaf_ .

> She forgot to take _____ . → She used _____ .

> She forgot to take _____ . → She used _____ .

> She forgot to take _____ . → She used _____ .

14 **(TIP)** **A verb is an action word. *Is*, *are* and *am* are verbs too.**
I *forgot* my umbrella when I *went* out. I *got* wet because it *was raining*.
Read Carol's story again. Circle six examples of verbs in the story.

Skills: *Writing*

15   Imagine a story about someone being resourceful. Make notes about what he/she did.

> Where was he/she? _____

What did he/she forget to take?	→	What did he/she use?
_____		_____

What did he/she forget to take?	→	What did he/she use?
_____		_____

What did he/she forget to take?	→	What did he/she use?
_____		_____

16 Write a story about someone being resourceful.

_____   _____
_____   _____
_____   _____
_____   _____
_____   _____
_____   _____
_____   _____
_____   _____
_____   _____
_____   _____
_____   _____

How do we **estimate** measurements?

1 **Match the pictures with the questions. Then match the questions and answers.**

a	b	c	d

1	How much orange juice is there?	C	**a**	There's about 5 litres.
2	How heavy is the rucksack?		**b**	It's about 6 kilograms.
3	How long is the torch?		**c**	There's about 100 millilitres.
4	How much water is there?		**d**	It's about 20 centimetres.

2 **This line shows the numbers 0–100 divided into tens. Estimate where the numbers in the box are on the line.**

~~15~~   32   50   67   75   98

3 **Estimate which numbers the arrows are pointing to on these lines.**

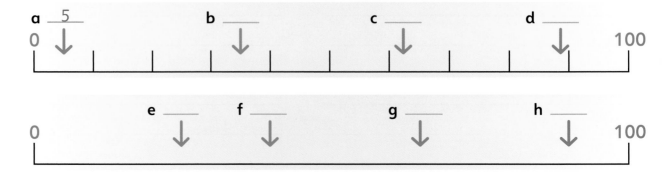

Evaluation

1 **Look at Mr Wood's *To do* list. Complete the Venn diagram.**

Mr. Wood's To do list	Andy	Sara	Tim	Pam	Dan
collect the torches		✓	✓		
put up the tents	✓	✓		✓	✓
wash the bowls			✓	✓	
cook the dinner		✓	✓		✓
dry the cups and plates	✓	✓		✓	✓
put away the blankets	✓		✓		✓

Dan

put up the tents

_____

Both

_____

_____

Tim

_____

_____

2 **Look at activity 1. Write the sentences.**

1   Mr Wood / ask / Sara and Tim

   Mr Wood asked Sara and Tim to collect the torches.

2   have to / the blankets

   _____

3   Mr Wood / ask / Tim and Pam

   _____

4   have to / the tents

   _____

3 **Complete the sentences about this unit.**

✓ = I can …   ✗ = I can't …

☐ **1** … name ten camping things.

☐ **2** … talk about what people *needed to, forgot to, tried to, had to do.*

☐ **3** … ask and answer *What did … ask … to do?* questions.

☐ **4** … talk about being resourceful.

☐ **5** … write a story about being resourceful.

6   The part of this unit I need to practise is _____ .

1 (Think) **Write the words. Then number the pictures.**

1 l y p a t t i s n n u m r e s _play instruments_

2 g l j e u g _____

3 d a e r t e r o y p _____

4 t p i n a a i r o s t r t p _____

5 k e a m l p u t u c r s e s _____

6 o d k s r t c i _____

 a | 1

 b

 c

 d

 e

 f

2 (Think) **Complete the table. Use the words in the box.**

> tell jokes   do acrobatics   street dance
> do tricks   play instruments   do cartwheels

Things people can do sitting down	Things people can't do sitting down
tell jokes	_____
_____	_____
_____	_____

3 (My World) **Complete the sentences about your friends and family.**

1 _____ is good at telling jokes.

2 _____ is good at playing an instrument.

3 _____ is good at _____ .

My picture dictionary ➔ Go to page 86: Write the new words.

4 **Look and complete the sentences.**

1 Sandra is _____*better than*_____ Jen at street dancing.

2 Dave is _____ at doing cartwheels.

3 Tom is _____ Sue at playing a musical instrument.

4 Tim is _____ at street dancing.

5 Matt is _____ than Joe at doing cartwheels.

5 **Look at activity 4. Write the sentences.**

1 *Jen is the worst at street dancing.* _____ (Jen / street dance)

2 _____ (Joe / Dave / do cartwheels)

3 _____ (Bea / play a musical instrument)

4 _____ (Sandra / Tim / street dance)

5 _____ (Tom / play a musical instrument)

6 **Complete the table about you and a friend. Then write sentences.**

	Better	Worse
Me		
My friend		

1 *I'm better than my friend at* _____ .

2 I'm worse _____ .

3 My friend _____ .

4 _____

7 **Look and answer the questions.**

1st Portraits Oliver 2nd Portraits Eva
3rd Portraits Bob 4th Portraits Rosa

1st Poetry Mandy 2nd Poetry Liam
3rd Poetry Pete 4th Poetry Cindy

1st Sculpture George 2nd Sculpture Nadia
3rd Sculpture Jake 4th Sculpture Nick

1 Who's better at reading poetry, Pete or Liam? _____ *Liam is.* _____

2 Who's the worst at making sculptures? _____

3 Who's better at painting portraits, Bob or Eva? _____

4 Who's the best at reading poetry? _____

5 Who's worse at making sculptures, Jake or Nadia? _____

8 **Look at activity 7 and write the questions. Use the words in brackets.**

1 *Who's the best at making sculptures?* _____ (best)
George is.

2 _____ (worse / Bob / Rosa)
Rosa is.

3 _____ (worst)
Cindy is.

4 _____ (better / Nadia / Nick)
Nadia is.

5 _____ (best)
Oliver is.

9 **Read and complete.**

Paula: You're very good at street dancing, Clara.

Clara: Thanks, but I'm not the [1]_____ *best* _____ in my family. My brother, Lucas, is
[2]_____ than me.

Paula: Who's [3]_____ at doing cartwheels, you or your brother?

Clara: My brother [4]_____ . He's very good, but he's [5]_____ than me
at doing acrobatics.

Paula: [6]_____ the best in your family at doing sport?

Clara: My sister [7]_____ . She plays basketball every Saturday morning.

Paula: Do you go with her?

Clara: No, I don't. I'm the [8]_____ in my family at waking up early. I always
want to sleep!

10 (Think) **Read the story again. Circle the correct words and then number.**

| 1 | The children follow _____ to the canoe. |
| | **a** an animal **b** (some footprints) **c** the map |

Jack stops the canoe safely away from the _____ .
a hippos **b** crocodiles **c** fish

Jack tries to slow the _____ down.
a river **b** canoe **c** hippos

They get in the canoe with the _____ and the compass.
a map **b** tent **c** river

11 **Read and correct the sentences.**

1 The children follow the very small footprints.

The children follow the very big footprints.

2 Jack finds the compass in a canoe.

_____

3 Sofia is the worst at reading the map.

_____

4 The children follow the river south.

_____

5 The children are scared of the fish in the water.

_____

12 (My World) **Write about two ways you showed the value: work together.**

1 *My sister and I made dinner together.*

2 _____

3 _____

Story Value **23**

Skills: *Reading*

13 Read Emily's email. Circle the correct words.

Hello Grandma,

I want to tell you about my new friend, Zoey. I met Zoey last month at dance class. We like going hiking together. We like going shopping together too. We do everything together! We are both friendly and talkative. We're both very clever too! Zoey is very artistic, she's ¹(better)/best at painting and making sculptures than I am, but I'm sportier than she is. I'm ²good/better at doing cartwheels and skateboarding than she is.

I'm ³better/best at playing musical instruments too. We had a talent show at school. The teacher asked Zoey and me to play the piano. When we played at the show, everyone was surprised! Zoey was the ⁴better/best, not me. Why? Zoey is more hardworking than I am. She practised every day but I didn't. I went skateboarding and rock climbing. I watched TV and played video games too. I was happy for her. Now I know that if you want to be the ⁵best/good, you have to work hard!

Love,

Emily

14 Look at activity 13. Read and write *true* or *false*.

1 Emily met Zoey at singing class. _____false_____

2 Zoey is better at painting than Emily. _____

3 Emily is better at making sculptures than Zoey. _____

4 Emily practised the piano every day but Zoey didn't. _____

5 Emily thinks that having fun is more important than working hard if you want to be the best. _____

15 (Think) Complete the table. Use the words in the box.

more artistic   clever   ~~sportier~~   friendly
better at skateboarding   better at painting

Emily	Zoey	Both
sportier	_____	_____
_____	_____	_____

16 (TIP) An adjective is a word that describes nouns.

Emily and Zoey are *friendly*.   The park is *big*.   The pencil is *new*.

Read Emily's email again. Circle the examples of adjectives.

Skills: *Writing*

17   **Make notes about you and a friend.**

My friend's name: _____

Where we met: _____

Things we like doing together: _____

Adjectives to describe us:

Me   Both   My friend

_____   _____   _____

_____   _____   _____

18   **Write an email about you and your friend.**

Hello _____,

_____

_____

_____

_____

_____

_____

_____

_____

_____

Love,

_____

What abilities do we need for physical activities?

1 Read and circle the correct words.

1 Some acrobats need **strength**/**speed** to lift other acrobats up in the air.
2 Runners and swimmers need **balance**/**speed** to win a race.
3 When we climb high mountains, we need **speed**/**stamina** to help us.
4 Ballet dancers and gymnasts need good **stamina**/**balance** to stand on one leg.

2 Write sentences about what we need for these physical activities.

1 *When we do cartwheels, we need balance.*

2 _____

3 _____

4 _____

5 _____

6 _____

3 Think of three physical activities you do. For each activity, write what you need: speed, strength, stamina or balance.

1 When I _____ I need _____ .

2 _____

3 _____

Evaluation

1 **Look and complete the sentences.**

Joe   Kevin   Tina

Frank   Mark

Penny

Simon

Anna   Sarah

1 Tina _____is worse at_____ _____making sculptures_____ than Kevin.

2 Joe is the _____ _____ making sculptures.

3 Frank _____ _____ than Penny.

4 Mark _____ _____ .

5 Sarah _____ _____ than Simon.

6 Anna _____ _____ .

2 **Complete the questions and answers.**

1 _____Who's better_____ at doing tricks, Mr Lee or Mr Jones?

Mr Jones _____ . He's very good.

2 _____ at reading poetry?

Jimmy _____ . He's not good at all.

3 _____ at telling jokes, your father or _____ ?

My mother _____ . She's really funny.

4 _____ at painting portraits?

Olivia _____ . Her portraits are beautiful.

5 _____ at doing cartwheels, _____ or your friend?

I _____ . I always fall down!

3 **Complete the sentences about this unit.**

✓ = I can …   ✗ = I can't …

☐ **1** … name ten talent show activities.

☐ **2** … compare using *better*, *best*, *worse* and *worst*.

☐ **3** … ask and answer questions comparing people.

☐ **4** … talk about working together.

☐ **5** … write an email comparing people.

6 The part of the unit I found the most useful was _____ .

Review 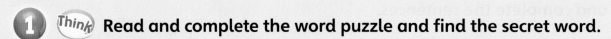 Units 1 and 2

1 (Think) **Read and complete the word puzzle and find the secret word.**

1 This helps us find places.
2 This is bad weather. Sometimes there's rain, thunder and lightning.
3 This is light in the sky in a storm.
4 This is the season before summer.
5 This helps us to see in the dark.
6 This is when there is too much water in streets and buildings.
7 We put this around bodies to keep warm.

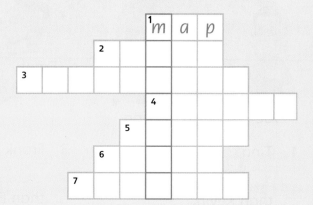

The secret word is _____

2 **Write sentences. Use the correct form of the verbs.**

1 when / Kevin / arrive / Florida / start / rain

When Kevin arrived in Florida, it started to rain.

2 John / forget / take / map / last weekend

_____

3 there / is / flood / last spring

_____

4 Larry / better / tell jokes / Henry

_____

5 Ms Hill / ask / students / wash / cups / yesterday

_____

6 who / worse / make sculptures / Jean / Sam?

_____

3 (Think) **Circle the odd one out.**

1 rucksack   sleeping bag   (drought)
2 winter   summer   storm
3 street dance   read poetry   tell jokes
4 thunder   autumn   lightning
5 do acrobatics   paint portraits   do cartwheels
6 torch   water bottle   cup

(Think) **Read and write the names.**

My name's Justin. Yesterday, my friends and I did a talent show. It was great! I told jokes because my friends say that I'm funny. Kat is the best at playing musical instruments. She played the guitar and sang. Eva read poetry, Andy did acrobatics and Fraser juggled. Paula is artistic. She painted a portrait of me!

Before the show, everyone was very nervous. We all talked a lot. Can you guess who said these sentences?

1 I need to find my book of poems.   _____*Eva*_____

2 Oh no! I forgot to bring my paintbrush!   _____

3 I have to make people laugh!   _____

4 I don't want to drop the balls.   _____

5 I need to have good balance.   _____

6 Shh! I'm trying to practise my song.   _____

5 (My World) **Answer the questions about you.**

1 Was there a drought in your country last summer?

_____

2 What do you need to do after school tomorrow?

_____

3 What did your mum ask you to do yesterday?

_____

4 Who is the worst at telling jokes in your family?

_____

5 Who is the best at doing cartwheels in your class?

_____

3 International food

1 Think Complete the words. Then tick (✓) the correct ingredients.

1 I like s t e w.

 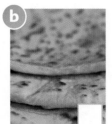 

a ✓   b   c ✓

2 I don't like __ u __ __ i.

a   b   c

3 I'd like to try __ oo __ __ e __ .

a   b   c

4 I often eat __ i __ __ a __ __ __ i __ __ .

a   b   c

2 Read and write the words.

1 These are from China. They're made with flour, meat and vegetables. _dumplings_

2 This food is from India. Sometimes it's yellow. It's made with meat and vegetables. _____

3 This food is from Mexico. It's made with flour, meat, cheese and vegetables. _____

4 This food is from Spain. It's got rice, vegetables and meat or fish. _____

5 This food is from Greece. It's made from meat and vegetables. _____

3 My World Which food is your country famous for? Name two.

1 My country is famous for _____ .

2 It's famous for _____ too.

 My picture dictionary → Go to page 87: Write the new words.

4 **Write sentences.**

1 I / my mum / make noodles for lunch / today

I want my mum to make noodles for lunch today.

2 Pablo / Ray / play football / yesterday

3 Our teacher / us / speak English / every day

4 Helen's dad / her / try / dumplings / last night

5 Jenny / Greg / play volleyball / every afternoon

5 **Read and correct the sentences.**

1 I wanted my mum to (made) some noodles.

I wanted my mum to make some noodles.

2 She wanted Zak try a kebab.

3 My sister wanted we to buy fish and chips.

4 Rick want me to make rice and beans for dinner.

5 We wanted our dad to bought tacos for lunch.

6 **What do your mum and dad want you to do? Write two things.**

1 My mum _____ .

2 My dad _____ .

7 Read and complete the sentences. Use the words in brackets.

1 I _____went_____ to the supermarket _____to buy_____ some rice. (go / buy)

2 I _____ some rice _____ some sushi. (buy / make)

3 I _____ some sushi _____ to a party. (make / take)

4 My friend Tina _____ a cake _____ our friend, Jake. (bake / give)

5 We all _____ to the party _____ a good time. (go / have)

8 Look and write sentences.

JAKE'S TO DO LIST
- ☑ Phone friends – invite them for dinner
- ☑ Go to the bookshop – buy a recipe book
- ☑ Go to the market – buy meat
- ☑ Buy flour – make dumplings
- ☑ Make a cake – have for dessert

LAURA'S TO DO LIST
- ☑ Catch a bus – go to town
- ☑ Go to the park – meet Anna
- ☑ Take a ball – play football
- ☑ Go to the shop – buy juice and crisps
- ☑ Go home – watch TV

1 Laura / buy juice and crisps
   Laura went to the shop to buy juice and crisps.

2 Jake / buy a recipe book
   _____

3 Laura / watch TV
   _____

4 Jake / buy meat
   _____

9 Look at activity 8. Answer the questions.

1 Why did Laura catch a bus?
   She caught a bus to go to town.

2 Why did Jake make a cake?
   _____

3 Why did Jake buy flour?
   _____

4 Why did Laura take a ball to the park?
   _____

5 Why did Jake phone his friends?

10 (Think) **Read the story again. Match and then number.**

1	The children are hungry but they __c__	**a**	yeti and forget the map and compass.
	They run away from the _____	**b**	vegetables and they cook an omelette.
	They find another _____	**c**	can't take the bird's eggs.
	They find more _____	**d**	egg near some onions.

11 **Answer the questions.**

1 Can the children take the animals' eggs?
   No, they can't.

2 What do they find in the basket?

   _____

3 Do they find some fruit?

   _____

4 What do they cook?

   _____

5 What do they forget?

   _____

12 (My World) **Think of four types of food you usually eat to show the value: eat healthy food.**

1 *I usually eat an apple at lunchtime.*

2 _____

3 _____

4 _____

5 _____

13 Read Steph's food blog. Then number the photos.

Steph the Chef

Last night my family and I went to my grandmother's house to enjoy a family dinner. Grandma wanted me to help her cook (because I'm Steph the Chef, of course!). We cooked a wonderful American dish called Macaroni Cheese. It's one of my favourite dishes. I want to share the recipe with you today.

Chef Steph Grandma's Easy, Cheesy Macaroni Cheese

1 box of pasta
1 egg
2 cups of milk
2 tablespoons of butter
2½ cups of cheese

Cook the pasta for 8 minutes. Mix the egg and milk. Add butter and cheese to the egg and milk. Put the pasta in a baking dish. Pour the egg, milk, butter, and cheese mixture on the pasta. Bake at 175 degrees for 30 to 40 minutes until the top is golden brown.

Mmmm. Serve the pasta with vegetables or a salad for an easy, delicious meal. Enjoy!

a

b

c

d

e   1

14 Look at activity 13. Answer the questions.

1 Where did Steph and her family go?

They went to Steph's grandmother's house.

2 What did Steph's grandmother want her to do?

3 What did they make?

4 Is it difficult to make?

5 What ingredients are in the recipe?

15 **TIP** When giving instructions, don't use *you*. Start the sentence with a verb.

✗ You mix the egg and the milk.
✓ Mix the egg and the milk.

Read Steph's blog again. Underline three sentences that give instructions.

Skills: *Writing*

16 Make notes about a recipe you like. Write the ingredients you need and then number the ingredients in the order you use them.

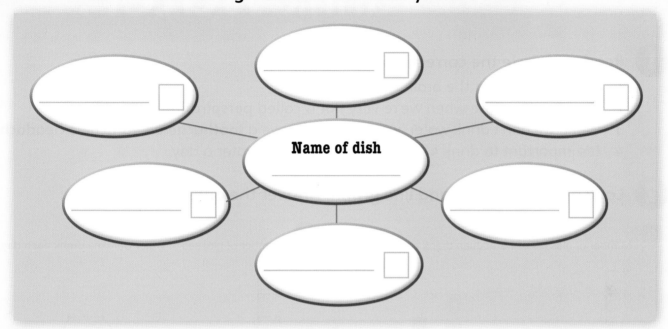

Name of dish

17 Write a food blog and include a recipe.

Why is it important to drink water?

1 **Read and circle the correct words.**

1 **Some/Most/All** of the brain is water.

2 The water we lose when we're very hot is called **perspiration/blood/skin**.

3 When we don't drink water, we sometimes have **a toothache/an earache/a headache**.

4 It's important to drink **4–6/6–8/8–10** glasses of water a day.

2 **Look at the bar chart and line graph. Answer the questions.**

a Number of glasses of water Juan drank each day.

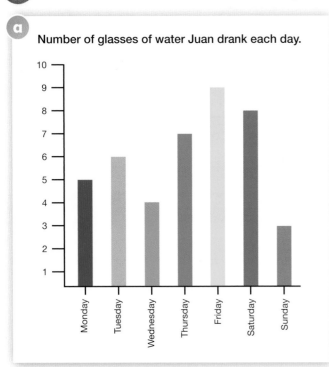

b Number of glasses of water Carolina drank each day.

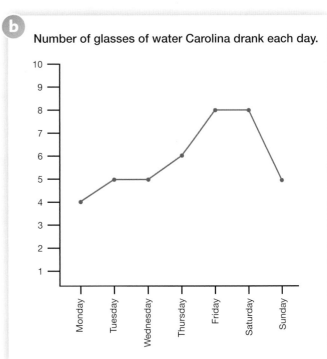

1 Who drank five glasses of water on Sunday? _Carolina_

2 Which day did Juan drink the most water? _____

3 Which day did Carolina drink six glasses of water? _____

4 Which day did the children drink the same number of glasses of water? _____

5 Who drank the most water this week? _____

3 **Look at activity 2. Write questions and ask a friend.**

1 Who drank _____ glasses of water on _____?

2 How many glasses of water _____?

3 _____

Evaluation

1 **Read and match.**

1 Ethan went to an Indian restaurant   b   **a** to learn to make kebabs.

2 Olivia bought rice   ☐   **b** to have curry.

3 Sandra went to a Greek cooking class   ☐   **c** to put in the tacos.

4 Oscar went to the supermarket   ☐   **d** to buy meat and vegetables for the stew.

5 Seth bought potatoes   ☐   **e** to make sushi.

6 Miguel cooked the meat   ☐   **f** to make fish and chips.

2 **Read and circle the correct answers.**

1 My mum wanted me to _____ .
   a made my bed   **b** (make my bed)

2 The boy went to the park _____ .
   a to go skateboarding   **b** to went skateboarding

3 Paul wanted his sister _____ .
   a make tacos for dinner   **b** to make tacos for dinner

4 My dad bought some flowers _____ .
   a to give to my mum   **b** to gave to my mum

5 The teacher wants her students to _____ .
   a study hard   **b** studied hard

6 May made dumplings and noodles _____ .
   a to took to the party   **b** to take to the party

7 My grandparents wanted us to _____ .
   a visit them last summer   **b** visited them last summer

3 **Complete the sentences about this unit.**

✔ = I can …   ✗ = I can't …

☐ **1** … name ten international foods.

☐ **2** … talk about people wanting someone to do something.

☐ **3** … talk about why someone did something using *to*.

☐ **4** … talk about eating healthy food.

☐ **5** … write a food blog with a recipe.

6 The part of this unit I enjoyed the most was _____ .

4 Music

1 Think **Look and write the words.**

> electric guitar   keyboard   flute   violin   ~~clarinet~~   trombone

1

Scott can play the
_____clarinet_____ .

2

Amy can play the
_____ .

3

Kai can play the
_____ .

4

Maria can play the
_____ .

5

Josh can play the
_____ .

6

Amelia can play the
_____ .

2 Think **Circle the odd one out.**

1 trumpet   saxophone   (keyboard)
2 violin   trombone   electric guitar
3 flute   cymbals   drums
4 clarinet   violin   flute

3 My World **What's your favourite and least favourite instrument?**

1 My favourite _____ .
2 My least favourite _____ .

My picture dictionary ➔ Go to page 88: Write the new words.

4 Complete the table.

Adjective	Adverb
loud	
quiet	
good	
bad	
beautiful	
quick	

5 Look and write sentences. Use the words in brackets.

1

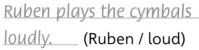

Ruben plays the cymbals loudly. (Ruben / loud)

2

_____ (Mel / beautiful)

3

_____ (Jen / quiet)

4

_____ (Joe / good)

5

_____ (Nina / bad)

6 My World Complete the sentences about you.

1 I _____ well.

2 I _____ quickly.

3 I _____ quietly.

7 **Read and complete the sentences. Use the words in brackets.**

1 Dan plays the drums ___more loudly___ than Leah does.

2 Jon plays _____ Ed does. (quickly)

3 Rosa _____ . (better)

4 May _____ . (beautifully)

5 Leah _____ . (quietly)

8 **Look at activity 7. Write the questions.**

1 _Who plays the keyboard more slowly, Jon or Ed?_ _____
   Ed does.

2 _____
   May does.

3 _____
   Sara does.

4 _____
   Dan does.

5 _____
   Rosa does.

9 **Complete the sentences about you.**

1 I play an instrument _____ than _____ does.

2 I run _____ than _____ does.

3 _____ does gymnastics _____ than I do.

4 _____ sings _____ than I do.

10 (Think) **Read the story again. Circle the correct words and then number.**

EMOCLEW

a It's an ocarina. **Jack/Ruby** tries to copy the tune.

b The yeti gives the children a **tablet/present**.

1 c Jack, Ruby and Sofia go back and find the (map)/**yeti** and the compass.

d The magic **tablet/ocarina** takes the children and the yeti away!

11 **Read and complete. Use the words in the box.**

> going ~~compass~~ ocarina slowly present yeti quickly

The children go back and get their map and ¹____compass____ . Then they see the

²_____ . He gives them a ³_____ . It's an ⁴_____ . Jack plays

the ocarina. He plays it ⁵_____ and then again more ⁶_____ . What's

happening? The children and the yeti are ⁷_____ away.

12 (My World) **What can you do to show the value: persevere?**

1 <u>You can practise a musical instrument</u>
  <u>every day.</u>

2 _____
  _____
  _____

3 _____
  _____
  _____

13 Read Devon's interview. Complete with the correct form of the words in brackets.

Devon Lee is a pupil at Oak School. He plays the violin in the school orchestra. He plays
¹ _beautifully_ (beautiful) now, but he didn't play very ² _____ (good) two years ago. We talked to Devon about it and this is what he said.

Interviewer: You play the violin very ³ _____ (good), Devon. Was it always easy for you?

Devon: No, it wasn't. Two years ago, I played very ⁴ _____ . (bad)

Interviewer: Really? Tell me about it.

Devon: The teacher asked me to play in a school concert when the other violin player moved to a different school. I was very worried because the other player played ⁵ _____ than I did. (beautiful)

Interviewer: What happened?

Devon: The kids in the orchestra helped me to practise for two weeks. They were great. I played very ⁶ _____ (good) at the concert. Those kids are my best friends now.

Interviewer: Wow. That's a great story, Devon. We all know friends can be a big help!

14 Look at activity 13. Read and write *true* or *false*.

1 Devon is very good at playing the violin. _true_

2 He always played the violin beautifully. _____

3 The other violin player left Devon's school. _____

4 The teacher helped Devon to practise for two weeks. _____

5 The children in the orchestra are now Devon's best friends. _____

15  **TIP** We know adjectives describe nouns. Adverbs describe verbs.

Adjective: John is *quick*.
Adverb: John runs *quickly*.

Read Devon's interview again. Circle three adverbs. Underline the verbs they describe.

Skills: *Writing*

  Make notes about someone who had a problem and a friend who helped.

| What was the person worried about? | How did the person's friend help? | What happened in the end? |

  Write an interview about someone who solved a problem with a friend's help.

How do string instruments make high and low sounds?

1 **Complete the sentences. Use the words in the box.**

> high   ~~vibrate~~   low   quickly   lower   higher

1 A string instrument makes a sound when the strings ____vibrate____ .

2 When something vibrates slowly, it makes a _____ sound.

3 When something vibrates quickly, it makes a _____ sound.

4 When we play a guitar, the thick strings make a _____ sound than the thin strings.

5 Short strings vibrate more _____ than long strings.

6 Short strings make a _____ sound than long strings.

2 **Look and answer the questions.**

1 Who is making a high-pitched sound?

____Katie____

2 Why is the sound higher?

Because the string is _____ .

3 Who is making a low-pitched sound?

_____

4 Why is the sound lower?

_____

_____

5 Alice makes the guitar string tighter. What happens to the sound it makes?

_____

_____

3 **In your notebook, design and write about a string instrument.**

Evaluation

1 **Read and complete. Use the correct form of the words in the boxes.**

> quiet   bad   ~~good~~

My name is Linda and I'm in the school band. I love music. I play the trombone and the trumpet. I play them very ¹_____*well*_____ . Everyone says I'm the best. I like to sing too, but I sing ²_____ . Sometimes our teacher asks me to sing more ³_____ !

> quick   slow   bad

I'm not very sporty. I always run very ⁴_____ . I never win a race. My best friend, Nick, runs more ⁵_____ than I do. And I'm ⁶_____ at playing football than all the other kids in my class!

> quiet   quick   loud

I'm very friendly and talkative. I talk more ⁷_____ than any of my friends. Sometimes they ask me to slow down. I talk very ⁸_____ , too. I must try to talk more ⁹_____ when I'm in the library or in class.

2 **Look at activity 1. Answer the questions.**

1 Does Linda play the trombone badly?   _No, she doesn't. She plays well._

2 What does Linda's teacher ask her to do?   _____

3 Does Linda run slowly?   _____

4 Who runs more quickly, Linda or Nick?   _____

5 Does Linda talk quietly and slowly?   _____

3 **Complete the sentences about this unit.**

✓ = I can …   ✗ = I can't …

☐ 1 … name ten musical instruments.

☐ 2 … talk about how someone does something.

☐ 3 … compare how people do things.

☐ 4 … talk about ways to persevere.

☐ 5 … write an interview.

6 The part of this unit I found the most interesting was _____ .

Review Units 3 and 4

1 (Think) **Read and write the words. Then find and circle.**

1 This food is meat and vegetables on a stick.
You can eat it in Greece. _kebabs_

2 You hold this instrument in your hands.
Then you hit the two parts together. _____

3 This is a Japanese dish with rice, fish
and vegetables. _____

4 This instrument is like a piano, but it's
smaller. _____

5 Part of this dish is from the ocean. The other
part is made of potatoes. _____

6 You blow into this instrument. It's bigger
than a trumpet. _____

7 This food is popular in Thailand, China and
Japan. It's like pasta. _____

8 You blow into this instrument. You hold it to
the side, not in front of you. _____

F	C	Y	M	B	A	L	S	X	D
I	W	L	W	T	G	E	H	D	U
S	O	H	Y	V	A	N	F	U	Y
H	P	Q	Z	L	S	O	L	G	Y
A	F	L	U	T	E	B	D	E	B
N	I	H	S	U	S	M	B	W	Y
D	O	K	E	Y	B	O	A	R	D
C	D	C	L	F	V	R	V	U	J
H	T	S	D	E	S	T	A	K	G
I	L	O	O	V	M	J	E	I	R
P	P	G	O	S	B	A	B	E	K
S	Q	H	N	F	W	H	P	Q	H

2 **Read and circle the correct answers.**

1 Jamie _____ Tom.
  a talks very quietly   **b** talks more quietly than   **c** talks quiet than

2 Our teacher _____ do our homework.
  a wanted us   **b** wants us to   **c** wants us

3 You play the saxophone _____ I do.
  a well than   **b** better than   **c** best than

4 Billie went to the supermarket _____ rice and fish.
  a to buy   **b** buy   **c** to bought

5 My sisters and I cooked the stew _____ .
  a very quickly   **b** very good   **c** very quick

3 **Read and complete the table.**

John, Sarah and Peter are in a band. Last night they went to a restaurant to have dinner after the concert. They each had a different dish. Read the clues. Which instrument does each person play? What did each person eat?

Clues:
1 Peter ate Japanese food.
2 The keyboard player and the electric guitar player are boys.
3 The electric guitar player didn't eat sushi.
4 Sarah doesn't like rice.

	drums	electric guitar	keyboard	sushi	paella	tacos
Peter				✓		
Sarah						
John						

4 **Answer the questions about you.**

1 What's your favourite international food?

2 What country is it from?

3 What did your teacher want you to do in English class today?

4 What did your friend want you to do yesterday?

5 Which musical instrument would you like to learn to play?

5 Now and then

1 (Think) **Read and complete the sentences.**

1　My dad reads the sports page in our city's ___newspaper___ every day.

2　When I don't know a word, I usually look it up in a _____ .

3　My friends and I like to play _____ on my laptop after school.

4　My mum bought a new _____ for her e-reader.

5　I wrote a _____ to my aunt last week, because she hasn't got a computer.

2 (Think) **Look and write the words in the table.**

Things that don't use electricity	Things that use electricity
a letter	_____
_____	_____
_____	_____

3 (My World) **How often do you use the things in activities 1 and 2?**

1　I never _____ .

2　I sometimes _____ .

3　_____ every day.

My picture dictionary ➡ Go to page 89: Write the new words.

4 Look and complete the sentences with *could* or *couldn't*.

1 Mary _____could_____ use an encyclopedia in 1970.
2 She _____ use the internet in 1970.
3 She _____ read an e-book in 2010.
4 She _____ write a letter in 1970.
5 She _____ play online games in 1970.

5 Look at activity 4. Write sentences about Mary.

1 check the weather on a website / 2010
   Mary could check the weather on a website in 2010.
2 use an encyclopedia / 1970
   _____
3 send an email / 1970
   _____
4 use the internet / 2010
   _____
5 read an e-book / 1970
   _____

6 Put the words in order.

1 an / My grandmother / couldn't / email / 1960. / send / in
   My grandmother couldn't send an email in 1960.
2 use / Your father / could / dictionary / young. / a / was / when / he
   _____
3 1995. / could / online / People / play / in / games
   _____
4 1980. / Sam's mother / read / e-books / in / couldn't
   _____
5 could / letters / 1970. / send / My grandfather / in
   _____

7 Look and answer the questions.

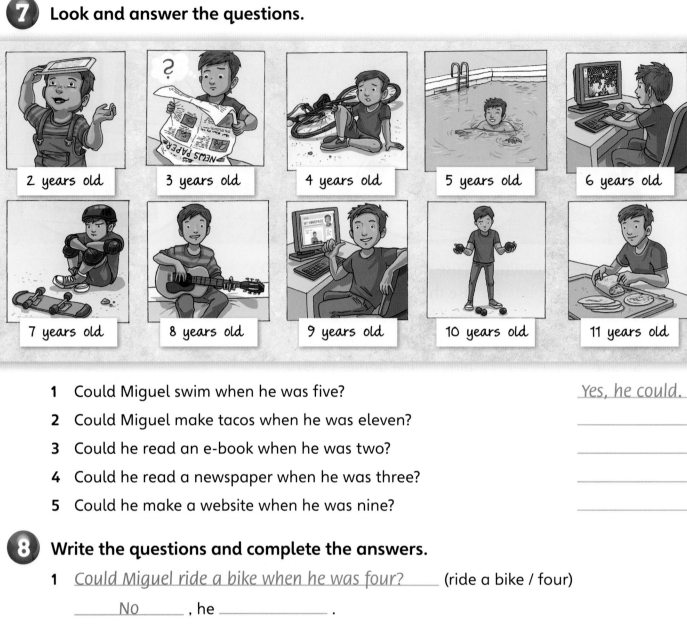

2 years old	3 years old	4 years old	5 years old	6 years old
7 years old	8 years old	9 years old	10 years old	11 years old

1 Could Miguel swim when he was five?   _Yes, he could._

2 Could Miguel make tacos when he was eleven?   _____

3 Could he read an e-book when he was two?   _____

4 Could he read a newspaper when he was three?   _____

5 Could he make a website when he was nine?   _____

8 Write the questions and complete the answers.

1 _Could Miguel ride a bike when he was four?_   (ride a bike / four)

  _____No_____, he _____ .

2 _____ (play online games / six)

  _____ , he _____ .

3 _____ (juggle / ten)

  _____ , he _____ .

4 _____ (skateboard / seven)

  _____ , he _____ .

9 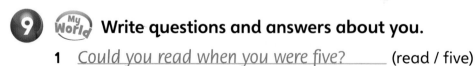 Write questions and answers about you.

1 _Could you read when you were five?_   (read / five)   _____

2 _____ (do cartwheels / nine)   _____

10 (Think) **Read the story again. Match and then number.**

☐ The children find ____

☐ Jack nearly sits ____

1 The children and the yeti climb __b__

☐ The yeti catches ____

a Ruby when she falls.

b in the snow and it's dangerous.

c a letter when the snake leaves.

d on a snake in the cave.

11 **Read and complete. Use the words in the box.**

rock   ~~mountains~~   Emoclew   cave   snowing   snake   Sofia   catches

The children and the yeti arrive in the ¹__mountains__ . It's dangerous because it's

windy and it's ²_____ . Ruby falls, but the yeti ³_____ her. The

children follow the yeti into a ⁴_____ . Jack thinks he's sitting down on a

⁵_____ , but it's a ⁶_____ ! When the snake goes away,

⁷_____ sees a letter. The address is in ⁸_____ . The children decide

to take the letter with them.

12 (My World) **What can you do to show the value: protect your friends?**

1 You can share your umbrella with your
friends when it rains.

2 _____
_____

3 _____
_____

Skills: *Reading*

13 **Read Robert's essay. Then look at the pictures and circle ☺ or ☹.**

Robert Simmons   The good and the bad of mobile phones

Everyone loves new technology. People want to buy the newest computers, tablets, mobile phones and other gadgets. But our grandparents couldn't call or text their friends on mobile phones. They couldn't look up information on computers or tablets. Are we happier now than they were then? I don't think so.

Mobile phones are great. We can phone our parents. We can call quickly for help in an emergency. We can text our friends and family. We can take pictures using our phones so we don't have to carry a camera around. We can even go online with smartphones to get directions or find a good restaurant.

But mobile phones aren't always great. We see people playing games or texting on their phones when they're with their family and friends. Why aren't they talking to each other? Some people drive and use their mobile phones and that's very dangerous. Some people walk and text at the same time. They sometimes fall and get hurt.

I think mobile phones are great but we must be careful we don't use them too much!

☺ ☹   ☺ ☹   ☺ ☹   ☺ ☹

14 **Look at activity 13. Complete the sentences.**

1 Robert thinks we're not happier now _than our grandparents were then_ .

2 We can use mobile phones to call quickly _____ .

3 We can also use mobile phones to find _____ .

4 Robert thinks people shouldn't play games or text when they're with

   _____ .

5 He thinks driving and _____ .

15 **(TIP) We join two sentences together using *or*. We use *or* when there's a choice.**

You can read the article in the newspaper. You can read the article online. →
You can read the article in the newspaper *or* online.

Read Robert's essay again. Underline the sentences that use *or* and circle the two choices in each sentence.

Skills: *Writing*

16 Make notes about a type of technology. Complete the table about the good and the bad things about it.

Type of technology _____

Good	Bad
_____	_____
_____	_____
_____	_____

17 Write an essay about the good and bad things about a type of technology.

Title: _____

_____
_____
_____
_____
_____
_____
_____
_____
_____
_____
_____
_____
_____
_____
_____
_____
_____
_____

What do primary sources tell us about life in the past?

1 Look and write the words under the pictures. Then tick (✓) the primary sources from Ancient Egypt.

> history book   ~~painting~~   board game   jewellery   tools   website   statue

a ✓

painting

b

c

d

e

f

g

2 Look at activity 1. Read and write the letters.

1 This tells us that the Egyptians liked to play games. `e`

2 This tells us that the Egyptians could make and play musical instruments.

3 This tells us that the Egyptians used tools for farming.

4 This tells us that the Egyptians wore beautiful objects.

5 This tells us that the Egyptians could make things from stone.

3 Imagine you see the primary sources from activity 1 in a museum. Choose two and write a question you can ask about each one.

1 _____

2 _____

Evaluation

1 **Read and complete with *could* or *couldn't*.**

My Uncle Bill is a clever man, but he isn't good at using technology. He tried to send an email, but he
[1] _couldn't_ turn on the computer. He tried to text my aunt, but he [2]_____ remember her mobile phone number. He tried to read an e-book, but he [3]_____ turn on his e-reader. He [4]_____ play online games on his tablet because I helped him. '[5]_____ you use a computer when you were young?' I asked him. 'No, Alice', he said. 'We [6]_____ use computers then because we didn't have them! But we [7]_____ read newspapers, magazines and send letters.' Now I know why Uncle Bill isn't good at using technology!

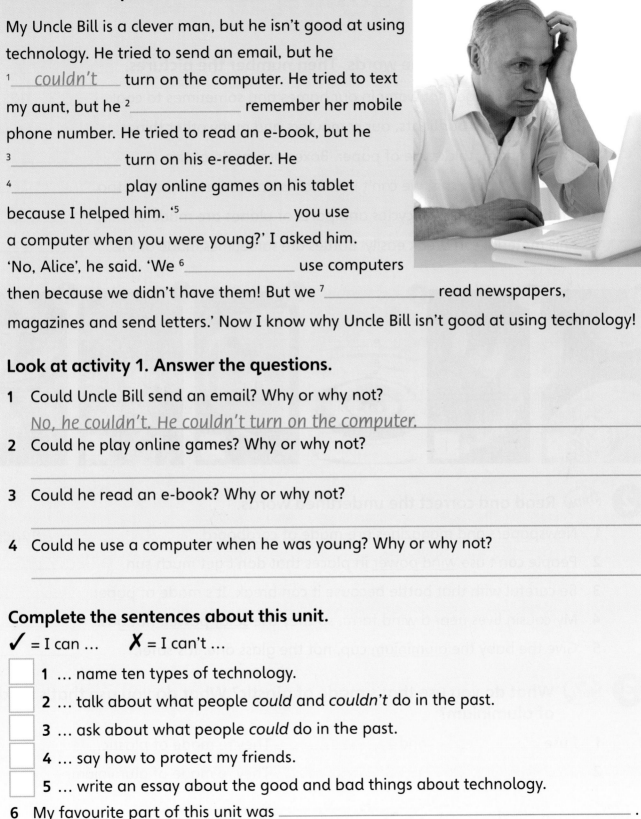

2 **Look at activity 1. Answer the questions.**

1 Could Uncle Bill send an email? Why or why not?
No, he couldn't. He couldn't turn on the computer.

2 Could he play online games? Why or why not?
_____

3 Could he read an e-book? Why or why not?
_____

4 Could he use a computer when he was young? Why or why not?
_____

3 **Complete the sentences about this unit.**

✓ = I can …   ✗ = I can't …

☐ **1** … name ten types of technology.

☐ **2** … talk about what people *could* and *couldn't* do in the past.

☐ **3** … ask about what people *could* do in the past.

☐ **4** … say how to protect my friends.

☐ **5** … write an essay about the good and bad things about technology.

6 My favourite part of this unit was _____ .

6 The environment

1 Think Read and write the words. Then number the pictures.

1 We use this to get hot water in our homes and sometimes to cook. _____gas_____

2 We use this for our lights, our computers and many other things. _____

3 This is a hard, thick type of paper. Boxes are made of this. _____

4 If we don't have this, we can't live. Plants and animals need it, too. _____

5 Drinks cans, parts of bicycles and parts of planes are made of this. _____

6 This material can break easily. Bottles are sometimes made of this. _____

a	b	c	d	e	f
	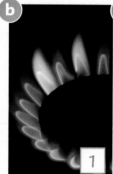				

2 Think Read and correct the underlined words.

1 Newspapers and magazines are made of <u>cardboard</u>. _____paper_____

2 People can't use <u>wind power</u> in places that don't get much sun. _____

3 Be careful with that bottle because it can break. It's made of <u>paper</u>. _____

4 My cousin lives near a wind farm, so they use <u>solar power</u>, not gas. _____

5 Give the baby the <u>aluminium</u> cup, not the glass one. It's safer. _____

3 My World What do you use that's made of plastic? What do you use that's made of aluminium?

1 I use _____ and _____ . They're made of plastic.

2 _____ . They're made of aluminium.

My picture dictionary → Go to page 90: Write the new words.

4 Read and complete the interview with *should* or *shouldn't*.

Baytown School news

Keep Baytown green

Kevin is the leader of the Baytown School Environment Club. Our reporter, Jenny, asked Kevin for some ideas for keeping Baytown green.

Jenny: Kevin, tell us about some things young people should do to help keep Baytown green.

Kevin: There are a lot of things we should do. We ¹_____*should*_____ recycle plastic, aluminium and paper. We ²_____ throw away newspapers, magazines and cardboard. We ³_____ recycle them.

Jenny: What about rubbish? There are some things that we can't recycle.

Kevin: Yes, Jenny, that's right. We ⁴_____ make a lot of rubbish, and we ⁵_____ use a lot of plastic bags, because we can't recycle them.

Jenny: But we can reuse plastic bags.

Kevin: Yes, we ⁶_____ reuse plastic bags when we can.

Jenny: Let's talk about other things we can do at home.

Kevin: Well, we ⁷_____ use a lot of water. We ⁸_____ reuse rainwater in our gardens.

Jenny: And we ⁹_____ waste electricity.

Kevin: Yes, we ¹⁰_____ turn off lights and computers when we aren't using them.

Jenny: How about outside of our homes?

Kevin: We ¹¹_____ ask our parents to drive us everywhere. We ¹²_____ walk or take the bus.

Jenny: Thank you for those great ideas Kevin. Now let's all work hard to keep Baytown green!

---

5 Read and write *true* or *false*.

1 Kevin is the school newsletter reporter. _____*false*_____

2 The name of the club is Baytown Student Green Club. _____

3 There aren't many things young people can do to help the environment. _____

4 We should reuse plastic bags. _____

5 People shouldn't leave their computers on all the time. _____

6 People should travel by car a lot. _____

6 **My World** Which of Kevin's ideas do you think are the most important? Name two.

1 I think we should _____ .

2 I think _____ .

7 Answer the questions. Then tick (✓) the correct picture.

1 What should we do to save water?

We should collect rainwater for
our gardens.

2 What should we do to save electricity?

3 What should we do to use less paper?

4 What should we do to reduce waste?

5 What should we do to save forests?

8 Complete the questions. Then circle the correct answers.

1 What _____ should we do _____ to save energy?
   a We should use solar energy.   **b** We should throw our rubbish in the rubbish bin.

2 What _____ save water?
   a We should recycle our cans.   **b** We should have showers, not baths.

3 What _____ paper?
   a We should write on both sides.   **b** We should use solar energy.

4 _____ waste?
   a We should reuse and recycle.   **b** We should do less homework.

5 _____ gas?
   a We should collect rainwater   **b** We should use less hot water.
   for our gardens.

9 (Think) **Read the story again. Correct the sentences and then number.**

[ ] **a** They follow the eagle to the rope mountain.

_____

[ ] **b** Sofia sees that the bridge is new and tells Jack. They fix it.

_____

[1] **c** The children pick up the ~~eagle~~ and take it with them.
  The children pick up the rubbish and take it with them.

[ ] **d** Jack helps the yeti and it flies away.

_____

10 **Read and match the questions and answers.**

1 Did the children pick up the rubbish?	[c]	**a** Yes, it is.
2 Who helped the eagle fly away?	[ ]	**b** They use a rope.
3 Where does the eagle take the children?	[ ]	**c** Yes, they did.
4 Is the bridge broken?	[ ]	**d** Jack did.
5 What do they use to fix it?	[ ]	**e** To the rope bridge.

11 (My World) **What can you do to show the value: reuse and recycle?**

1 *You can recycle newspapers and*
  magazines.

2 _____

  _____

3 _____

  _____

12 Read Kerry's blog. Write the words under the pictures.

Go green with Kerry!

Hey everybody! We all know we should reduce waste, reuse and recycle. We know we shouldn't throw away old things if we can use them again. So I have a great message board you can make with ugly, old things. Here's what you need:

- A baking tray
- A hammer and a nail
- Wrapping paper
- Scissors
- Glue
- An empty can
- Bottle tops
- Notepaper
- Magnets

1 Ask your mum or dad to make a hole in one end of the baking tray with a hammer and a nail.

2 Measure and cut the wrapping paper to fit the baking tray. Glue the wrapping paper to the baking tray.

3 Measure and cut the wrapping paper to fit the can. Glue the wrapping paper to the can. Glue two magnets to the side of the can. Put the can on the baking tray for pens and pencils.

4 Glue magnets inside the bottle tops. Cover the front with notepaper. Put your board on the wall.

And there you have it! A beautiful, new message board! Visit my blog next time for ideas about saving energy.

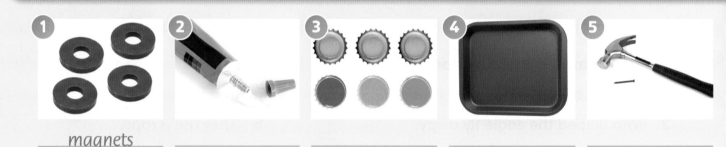

___magnets___ _____ _____ _____ _____

13 Look at activity 12. Put the sentences in order.

	a	Stick pretty wrapping paper on the baking tray and the can with glue.
	b	Put your message board on the wall.
1	c	Find an old baking tray and an aluminium can.
	d	Put magnets on bottle tops and put them on the board.
	e	Ask for help to make a hole in one end of the baking tray.

14 **(TIP)** **Antonyms are words that have opposite meanings.**

We had *good* weather on holiday. It was sunny every day.

We had *bad* weather on holiday. It rained every day.

Read Kerry's blog again. Circle the examples of antonyms.

Skills: *Writing*

15 **Make notes about something you can make by reusing old things.**

What can you make? _____

What do you need? _____

Circle the verbs you need to use in your writing: find, put, measure, cut, glue, make a hole, cover

Make notes about how you make it:

_____

_____

_____

_____

_____

16 **Write a blog about reusing things to make something new.**

_____

_____

_____

_____

_____

_____

_____

_____

_____

_____

_____

_____

What happens to our old glass bottles?

1 **Look and write the words under the pictures.**

furnace   recycling bin   green glass   clear glass   ~~melted glass~~   sand

melted glass

2 **Put the sentences in order.**

	a	A big lorry comes and takes our old glass bottles away.
	b	They use the melted glass to make new bottles.
	c	The clear glass, green glass and brown glass go in different groups.
1	d	We put our glass bottles in a recycling bin.
	e	Shops sell the recycled glass bottles.
	f	The glass melts.
	g	They put the glass and sand in a furnace.
	h	Machines break the glass and mix it with sand.

3 **How much glass, plastic, aluminium and paper do you recycle each week?**
Make a bar chart.

Evaluation

1 **Read and complete. Use the words in the box.**

> shouldn't   cardboard   electricity   ~~aluminium~~   should   water   plastic   glass

Mandy's room is a mess! There are [1] *aluminium* cans on the desk. There are [2]_____ bottles under the desk. There are [3]_____ bags under the bed. There are newspapers and magazines on the floor near a big [4]_____ box. She should recycle the cans and bottles. She [5]_____ recycle the newspapers and magazines, too. Her computer and desk lamp are on. She should turn them off to save [6]_____ . Mandy is in the bathroom now. She is having a long bath. She should have showers to save [7]_____ . And she [8]_____ be so messy!

2 **Read activity 1. Answer the questions.**

1 What should Mandy do with the cans and bottles?
   She should recycle the cans and bottles.
2 What should Mandy do to save paper?

   _____

3 What should Mandy do to save electricity?

   _____

4 What should Mandy do to save water?

   _____

3 **Complete the sentences about this unit.**
✓ = I can …   ✗ = I can't …

☐ **1** … name ten words about the environment.
☐ **2** … talk about what people *should* and *shouldn't* do.
☐ **3** … ask about what people *should* do.
☐ **4** … say how to reuse and recycle.
☐ **5** … write a blog about making something new from recycled things.
6 The part of this unit I found most useful was _____ .

Review Units 5 and 6

1 (Think) **Read and complete the word puzzle.**

Across

2 This is a book of words.
5 A lot of bags are made from this.
6 We play this on the computer.
7 This is a big book with a lot of information.
9 We read this on a tablet or an e-reader.

Down

1 This gives us light at night.
3 This comes from trees.
4 This is what we use when we go online.
8 We need this to live.

2 **Read and circle the correct answers.**

1 Lisa couldn't _____ because it was broken.
   a   reused the plastic bag   b   (reuse the plastic bag)

2 Phillip shouldn't _____ .
   a   play online games all day   b   played online games all day

3 _____ you use a computer when you were young? No, I _____ .
   a   Could, could   b   Could, couldn't

4 What _____ we do to save paper? We _____ write on both sides.
   a   should, should   b   should, shouldn't

5 When my dad was at school, he _____ use an encyclopedia, but he _____ look for the information on the internet.
   a   couldn't, couldn't   b   could, couldn't

6 _____ you swim when you were six? No, but I _____ swim well now.
   a   Could, couldn't   b   Could, can

3 (Think) **Read and match the questions and answers.**

1 Could you read when you were three? **d**

2 My grandma hasn't got a computer, so I can't send her emails. ☐

3 Could you use a computer when you were six? ☐

4 I don't like going to bed early, but I'm always tired in the morning. ☐

5 Could you speak English when you were seven? ☐

6 I like doing sport outside in summer, but I sometimes feel tired and get a headache. ☐

a No, I couldn't, but I could understand a little.

b You should drink a lot of water when you do exercise.

c You should send her letters.

d No, I couldn't, but I liked looking at the pictures.

e You shouldn't play online games late at night.

f I could turn it on, but I couldn't use the internet.

4 (My World) **Answer the questions about you.**

1 What technology do you use the most at home?

_____

2 Write two things you could do when you were four.

_____

_____

3 Write two things you couldn't do when you were six.

_____

_____

4 What types of energy do you use at home – electricity, gas, solar energy or wind energy?

_____

5 What things do you usually recycle?

_____

6 What things do you usually reuse?

_____

7 Space

1 (Think) Read and write the words. Then number the pictures.

1 We live on the planet _____Earth_____ .

2 An _____ travels into space.

3 There are eight _____ in our solar system.

4 Astronauts travel to space in a _____ .

5 The sun is a big _____ .

6 Neil Armstrong was the first man on _____ .

| r | t | E | h | a |

| t | t | r | n | s | a | a | o | u |

| e | a | t | l | p | s | n |

| t | f | r | s | c | p | c | a | e | a |

| r | t | a | s |

| h | e | t | | o | m | n | o |

a

b

c

d

e

f

1

2 (Think) Circle the odd one out.

1 Earth   (spacecraft)   Mars

2 spacecraft   spacesuit   Earth

3 astronaut   planets   stars

4 the moon   Mars   Earth

5 space station Mars   space laboratory

3 (My World) What did you see in the sky last night? What didn't you see?

1 I saw _____ .

2 I didn't see _____ .

 My picture dictionary → Go to page 91: Write the new words.

4 Look at Andy and Amy's calendar for next week. Complete the sentences.

Monday	Tuesday	Wednesday	Thursday	Friday
Andy and Amy: ~~Go to the cinema~~ Start space mission	Amy: Take photos of Earth Andy: Tidy up the spacecraft	~~Have a day off~~ Andy and Amy: Arrive at the space station	Andy: Do experiments in the space laboratory Amy: Work outside the space station	Amy: Clean the spacesuits Andy: Have an interview with NASA

1 Andy _____isn't going to_____ have an interview with NASA on Wednesday.

2 Amy _____ take photos of Earth on Tuesday.

3 Andy _____ tidy up the spacecraft on Friday.

4 Andy and Amy _____ arrive at the space station on Wednesday.

5 Look at activity 4. Write the sentences.

1 Andy / Tuesday

Andy is going to tidy up the spacecraft on Tuesday. He isn't going to take photos of Mars.

2 Amy / Thursday

_____

_____

3 Andy and Amy / Monday

_____

_____

4 Andy / Thursday

_____

_____

5 Amy / Friday

_____

_____

6 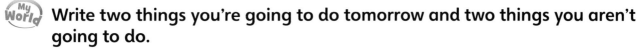 Write two things you're going to do tomorrow and two things you aren't going to do.

1 I'm going to _____ .

2 I'm _____ .

3 I'm not _____ .

4 _____

7 Put the words in order. Then circle the correct answers.

1 you / to / going / go / to / space camp? / Are

Are you going to go to space camp?

   a Yes, I do.   **b** (Yes, I am.)

2 going / he / do / is / at / What / to / the / space station?

_____

   a He's going work outside.   **b** He's going to work outside.

3 to / the / climb / they / Are / going / Mars climbing wall?

_____

   a No, they aren't.   **b** Yes, they did.

4 about / going / she / learn / Is / to / space missions?

_____

   a Yes, she going to.   **b** Yes, she is.

5 going / astronauts? / to / Are / meet / you

_____

   a No, you aren't.   **b** No, we aren't.

8 Look and answer the questions.

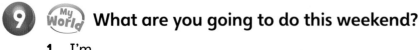

1 What is George going to do this weekend?

He's going to bake a cake.

2 Is Abby going to bake a cake this weekend?

_____

3 What is she going to do?

_____

4 Is Sam going to play on the computer this weekend?

_____

5 What is Christine going to do this weekend?

_____

9 **My World** What are you going to do this weekend?

1 I'm _____ .

2 _____

10 (Think) **Read the story again. Circle the correct words and then number.**

☐ They find a _____ with the letter *W* on it.
   a (wheel)   **b** map   **c** tree

☐ They find the _____ under the star and look under it.
   a tablet   **b** wheel   **c** tree

☐ They all think and try to guess the _____ .
   a letter   **b** password   **c** number

1 The children look up at the _____ to find the brightest star.
   a city   **b** sky   **c** forest

11 **Circle the mistakes and write the correct words.**

1 Ruby is pointing to the (biggest) star in the sky.   *brightest*

2 A red wheel is under the tree, coming out of the ground.   _____

3 The children need the map to enter the city of Emoclew.   _____

4 There are five gaps on the wheel for the other letters.   _____

5 The children know that the letter *C* is important.   _____

12 (My World) **When do you show the value: think logically?**

1 *You think logically when you solve*
maths problems.

2 _____

_____

3 _____

_____

Skills: *Reading*

13 **Read David's comic story. Circle the correct words.**

1 I'm going to be ¹a spacesuit/ an astronaut . I'm learning to fly a ²spacecraft/space station and float in zero gravity, because soon I'm going to travel into space.

2 It's important to exercise in space, so I'm going to take a running machine. I'm ³going/go to take my dog Max and my laptop, too. I wonder, is there internet in space?

3 Max and I ⁴am/are going to go for a walk on the moon every day. We're going to get rock samples and then work in the ⁵Earth/space laboratory.

4 We're going to see big rocks ⁶floating/walking in space. We're going to break the biggest ⁷rocks/stars with lasers, so they can't come down to Earth. We're going to save our ⁸sun/planet!

14 **Look at activity 13. Answer the questions.**

1 Is David going to be an astronaut?

   Yes, he is.

2 What is he doing to prepare?

3 What is he going to take?

4 Where are they going to work?

5 What are they going to do to the big rocks?

15 **TIP** **Some words are both verbs and nouns.**

The bird can *fly*. – There's a *fly* on the window.

I *walk* to school. – My mum and I go for a *walk* every evening.

My brother likes to *exercise*. – That's a difficult *exercise*.

Read David's comic story again. Find and circle *fly*, *walk* and *exercise*.

Are they verbs or nouns?

Skills: *Writing*

16 **Imagine you're going to travel to space. Make notes about your trip.**

What are you going to do to prepare?	
What are you going to take?	
What are you going to do in space?	
How are you going to help the people on Earth or other planets?	

17 **Write a comic story about your trip to space. Draw pictures.**

How are the planets different?

1 **Look and complete the words.**

1 the s u n 2 _ e _ c _ r _ 3 E _ _ t _

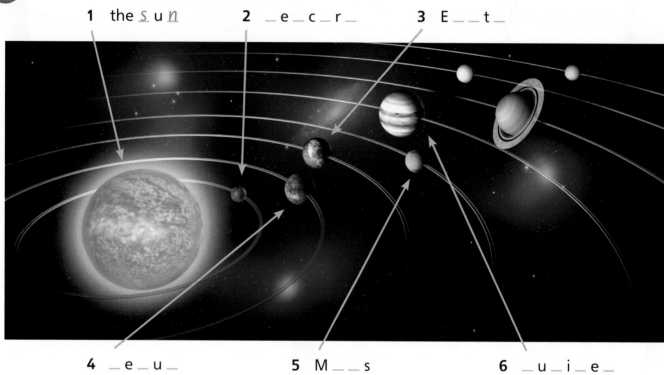

4 _ e _ u _ 5 M _ _ s 6 _ u _ i _ e _

2 **Read and write the words from activity 1.**

1 It's the planet we live on. _____Earth_____

2 It's the biggest planet in our solar system. _____

3 It's the smallest planet in our solar system. _____

4 It's the nearest planet to Earth. _____

5 It's one of the rock planets and it's fourth in our solar system. _____

6 All the planets orbit it. _____

3 **Write sentences about our solar system. Use the words in the box.**

| is   has got   moves   is made of   there are |

1 Jupiter is made of gas. _____

2 _____

3 _____

Evaluation

1 **Look at the timeline. Write sentences.**

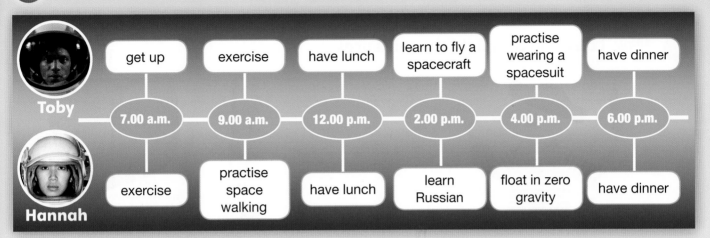

1 Toby / zero gravity / four o'clock

Toby isn't going to float in zero
gravity at four o'clock.

3 Toby and Hannah / lunch / twelve o'clock

_____

_____

2 Hannah / spacesuit / four o'clock

_____

_____

4 Hannah / Russian / six o'clock

_____

_____

2 **Look at activity 1. Answer the questions.**

1 Is Toby going to get up at 12.00 p.m.?   *No, he isn't.*

2 Is Toby going to exercise at 9.00 a.m.?   _____

3 Is Hannah going to learn Russian at 2.00 p.m.?   _____

4 Are Toby and Hannah going to have dinner at 8.00 p.m.?   _____

3 **Complete the sentences about this unit.**

✓ = I can …   ✗ = I can't …

☐ **1** … name ten words about space travel and space.

☐ **2** … talk about what people are *going to* do in the future.

☐ **3** … ask about what people are *going to* do in the future.

☐ **4** … talk about ways to think logically.

☐ **5** … write a comic story about space travel.

6 My favourite part of this unit was _____ .

8 Celebrations

1 (Think) **Look and complete the sentences.**

1 A ___pirate___ doesn't wear a mask.

2 My uncle is a very good _____ .

3 Rebecca's going to be a _____ in a carnival parade.

4 A _____ makes people laugh.

2 **Read and complete the sentences.**

1 When you put this on, no one can see your face. It's a ___mask___ .

2 This is an animal you can see and read about in story books. It's a _____ .

3 These are beautiful colourful lights in the dark sky. They're _____ .

4 There are fun, scary rides at this place. It's a _____ .

5 This is big and beautiful and people stand on it in a parade. It's a _____ .

6 Dancers, clowns and pirates wear this in a parade. It's a _____ .

My picture dictionary Go to page 92: Write the new words.

3 **Look and complete the sentences with *who, which* or *where*.**

1 This is the park ____where____ we have
a carnival in our town every year.

2 These are the musicians _____
play the music.

3 These are the fireworks _____
we see in the sky at night.

4 These are the floats _____
are in the parade.

5 This is the street _____
we watch the parade.

6 These are the dancers _____
dance on the floats.

4 **Put the words in order.**

1 where / we / the funfair / went on / rides. / This is
This is the funfair where we went on rides.

2 a pirate. / man / He's / who / the / dressed up / as
_____

3 the most. / I / float / That's / which / like / the
_____

4 there's / the town / where / This is / carnival / a big / every year.
_____

5 the / She's / makes / woman / who / masks. / the
_____

5 **Join the two sentences using *who, which* or *where*.**

1 This is the clarinet. I played it in the talent show.
This is the clarinet which I played in the talent show.

2 This is the town. There was a bad storm last night.
_____

3 This is the astronaut. He's going to fly the spacecraft.
_____

4 These are the dumplings. My mother cooked them for me.
_____

5 It's the costume. My uncle made it for the parade.
_____

6 **Look and complete the questions and answers.**

A: Is this your cousin
_____who_____ lives in Italy?

B: _____ , it _____ .
I haven't got any cousins
in Italy.

A: Is this the hotel _____
you stayed?

B: _____ , it _____ .
Of course not.

A: Is this the cake _____
your aunt baked for your
birthday?

B: _____ , it _____ .
It was delicious!

A: Is this the funfair
_____ your uncle
took you?

B: _____ , it _____ .
It was a lot of fun.

A: Is this your aunt
_____ lives in the
United Kingdom?

B: _____ , it _____ .
That's my mum!

7 **Write questions and answers.**

1 funfair / there are scary rides

Is this the funfair where there are scary rides? ✓ _Yes, it is._

2 friend / good at street dancing

_____ ✗ _____

3 costume / you wore in the play

_____ ✓ _____

4 restaurant / Tim had lunch

_____ ✓ _____

5 teacher / teaches you English

_____ ✗ _____

8 (Think) **Read the story again. Circle the correct words and then number.**

- [ ] **a** They have a lot of fun with the yetis at their **party/parade**.
- [ ] **b** The children find another word clue on the **street sign/door** and go back home.
- [ ] **c** They enter the competition and their **password/game** wins!
- [1] **d** The children find the password (Welcome)/**Go home** and enter the yeti city.

9 **Read and complete. Use the words in the box.**

> door   streets   ~~lost~~   competition   envelope   yeti   great   home   friends

When Ruby enters the password, the doors to the ¹_____lost_____ city open. The
²_____ is happy to be home. The yetis in the city welcome the children and the
yeti with a party. They all have a ³_____ time. When the children dance down
the ⁴_____ of the lost city, they see a sign that says Emoh Og. That's the street
on the ⁵_____ . They find number 3 and go in the open ⁶_____ .
They're ⁷_____ again and the game is finished. Sofia enters the computer
game ⁸_____ and she wins! She shares the prize with her ⁹_____ .

10 (My World) **Write about two times when you showed the value: share success with your friends.**

1 *I shared success with my friends*
   when we won the football match.

2 _____
   _____

3 _____
   _____

Story   Value   **77**

11 **Read Tara's email. Then number the pictures.**

Hello Lucy,

We're on holiday in the United States. We're staying with my cousins, Lily and John. They're the cousins who live in Florida. I'm having a great time. You can see the photos which we took at Super Fun Park in this email. Super Fun Park is the place where we had a party for my birthday last Saturday. We had a great time. The rides were scary, but they were fun. My favourite ride was the roller coaster.

We had hot dogs, hamburgers and a big chocolate birthday cake for lunch. Then we went to the water park. It was a hot day, but the water was cold! John and I went down the water slide ten times! John can swim, but Lily can't, so we didn't stay there for a long time.

That night, there was a parade with musicians and dancers and then amazing fireworks. I fell asleep in the car on the way home. I was tired, but I was happy. It was the best birthday ever!

See you next week.

Love,

Tara

1

12 **Look at activity 11. Circle the mistakes. Then write the sentences correctly.**

1 Tara is staying in Florida with her (friends,) Lily and John.

   Tara is staying with her cousins, Lily and John.

2 They celebrated Lily's birthday at Super Fun Park.

   _____

3 They had pizza, hamburgers and chocolate cake for lunch.

   _____

4 They didn't stay long at the water park because John can't swim.

   _____

5 There was a carnival with dancers and musicians that night.

   _____

13 **(TIP)** **Use *but* to join two sentences together with opposite ideas.**

The box is big. It's not heavy. – The box is big, *but* it's not heavy.

You're happy. I'm not happy. – You're happy, *but* I'm not.

Read Tara's email again. Underline the sentences with *but*.

Skills: *Writing*

14 Make notes about a celebration or a visit to a theme park, a funfair or a carnival on the chart.

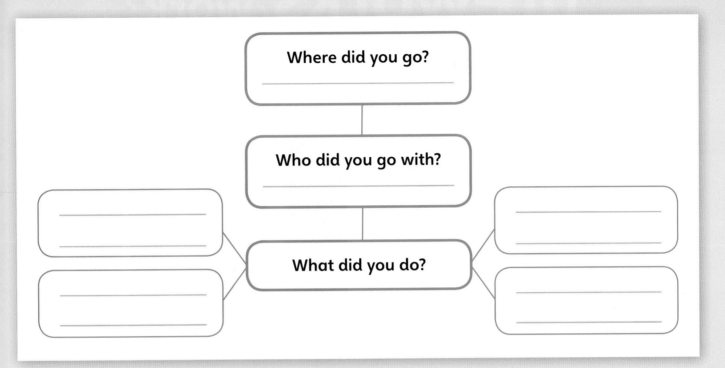

Where did you go?

_____

Who did you go with?

_____

What did you do?

15 Write an email about a celebration or a visit to a theme park, funfair or carnival.

Dear _____ ,

_____

_____

_____

_____

_____

_____

_____

Love,

_____

How do fireworks work?

1 **Look and write the words from the box.**

> fuse gunpowder ~~metal salts~~ lithium sodium copper

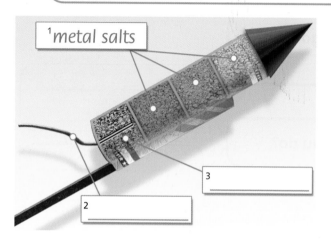

¹metal salts

3 _____

2 _____

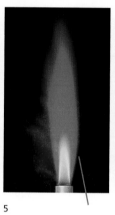

4 _____

5 _____

6 _____

2 **Read and complete the sentences. Use the words in the box.**

> metal salts gas ~~fuse~~ sound air gunpowder explodes

Someone lights the
¹_____fuse_____
so the
²_____
burns.

3 _____
makes the firework go
up into the
4 _____ .

The gunpowder
5 _____
and makes a loud
6 _____ .

Different kinds of
7 _____
inside the firework
make bright lights in
different colours.

3 **Plan a celebration.**

What are you going to celebrate?

_____

When and where are you going to have the celebration?

_____

What are you going to do?

_____

Evaluation

1 Read and complete.

1

This is the parade ¹ _which_ our town has every summer. And that's me! My name is Tim. I'm the boy ² _____ looks like a pirate. That's the costume ³ _____ my mum made for me.

2

That's the place ⁴ _____ they keep the floats. My favourite float is the one ⁵ _____ looks like a dragon. Those dancers have masks ⁶ _____ look beautiful.

3

These are the musicians ⁷ _____ play the music. The man ⁸ _____ plays the drum is my dad. That's the float ⁹ _____ they always play.

4

After the parade, there's a funfair ¹⁰ _____ we can go on rides and buy delicious things to eat. This is also the place ¹¹ _____ we have fireworks at night. It's great!

2 Look at activity 1. Answer the questions.

1 Is Tim the boy who is dressed up as a clown?   _No, he isn't._

2 Is he wearing a costume which his mum made?   _____

3 Is Tim's favourite float the one which looks like a pirate?   _____

4 Is the man who plays the drum Tim's uncle?   _____

3 Complete the sentences about this unit.

✓ = I can …   ✗ = I can't

☐ 1 … name ten things you sometimes see at celebrations.

☐ 2 … talk about people, places and things using *who*, *where* and *which*.

☐ 3 … ask about people, places and things using *who*, *where* and *which*.

☐ 4 … talk about how you share success with your friends.

☐ 5 … write an email about a celebration at a fun place or event.

6 The part of this unit I found most interesting was _____ .

Review Units 7 and 8

1 (Think) **Complete the sentences. Then find and circle the words.**

1 There are eight _____planets_____ in our solar system.

2 There's a _____ with a parade and a funfair in our town every year.

3 We can see many beautiful _____ on a clear, dark night.

4 That _____ has a red nose, wears a colourful costume and is very funny.

5 It's not easy for an astronaut to learn how to fly a _____ .

6 In China, people think the _____ is a lucky animal.

7 An astronaut has to wear a _____ when he's outside the spacecraft.

8 If you wear a _____ , people aren't going to know who you are.

P	Q	C	L	O	C	K	K	M	V
L	W	A	Y	T	L	U	C	X	S
A	D	R	A	G	O	N	Z	V	P
N	A	N	F	B	W	G	M	E	A
E	N	I	K	C	N	F	I	R	C
T	C	V	H	A	F	Q	M	R	E
S	E	A	P	B	S	T	A	R	S
X	W	L	S	I	H	W	S	P	U
Z	D	A	S	T	O	N	K	J	I
S	P	A	C	E	C	R	A	F	T

2 **Complete the sentences. Use *going to*, *who*, *where* or *which*.**

1 He's the astronaut _____who_____ walked on the moon.

2 The musicians aren't _____ play their instruments in the parade today.

3 That's the spacecraft _____ took the astronaut to Mars last year.

4 I'm _____ go to the carnival with my grandparents next weekend.

5 My friends are _____ eat space food at space camp.

6 That's the planet _____ they sent the Curiosity rover.

3 (Think) **Circle the odd one out.**

1 space station   spacecraft   space laboratory   the moon

2 spacesuit   costume   Mars   mask

3 funfair   musician   astronaut   dancer

4 funfair   space laboratory   pirate   carnival

5 spacesuit   fireworks   stars   the moon

4 **Think** **Read and complete the table.**

Ruben, Evie and Leo are going to go to their friend Marco's birthday party. They're going to wear costumes. Each person is going to wear a different costume. They've each got a different birthday present for Marco. Read the clues. Which costume is each person going to wear? Which present is each person going to give Marco?

Clues:

1 Evie is going to wear a spacesuit.
2 Ruben's present for Marco is going to help him to see when it's dark.
3 The astronaut isn't going to give Marco juggling balls.
4 The person who's going to wear a pirate costume isn't going to give Marco a torch.

	astronaut	pirate	clown	skateboard	torch	juggling balls
Ruben			✓			
Evie						
Leo						

5 **My World** **Answer the questions about you.**

1 Would you like to be an astronaut? Why or why not?

2 Would you like to go to space camp?

3 Are you going to go to school tomorrow?

4 What are you going to do for your next birthday?

5 Would you like to go to a carnival? Why or why not?

6 Is there a funfair or a parade in your town?

Seasons and weather

autumn

blanket

do acrobatics

curry

4 Music

clarinet

88 My picture dictionary

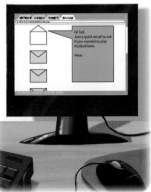

dictionary

aluminium

7 Space

astronaut

clown

Story fun

1 Who said it? Read and write the names.

Jack   Ruby   Sofia

1 _____Sofia_____   It's a wheel!

2 _____   Emoclew! We're in my game!

3 _____   Be careful, Ruby. It's dangerous.

4 _____   This is our egg!

5 _____   Oh dear! There's a lot of lightning.

6 _____   I know! It's *Welcome*! Emoclew backwards!

7 _____   I can paddle.

8 _____   I think you have to copy the tune.

9 _____   Wait, Jack! The bridge is broken.

2 Look at the pictures and write the values.

> Work together.   Reuse and recycle.   Persevere.
> ~~Be resourceful.~~   Eat healthy food.   Protect your friends.

1

Be resourceful.

2

3

4

5

6

3 Complete the word puzzle with the clues from the story.

Across

1 Now it's time for you to look for a clue that you can cook. In a nest is a tasty treat, but someone else wants to eat.

2 Follow the footprints to a canoe. Inside it is your second clue. North, south, east or west. This item always knows where's best.

3 The sixth clue is the strongest bird, but you should help it - it is hurt. Rescue it from a rope trap, and find a short cut on the map.

4 The fifth clue is something you send to give your news to a friend. Pick this up and take it with you on your journey to Emoclew.

Down

5 Guess the password and all of you can enter the city of Emoclew.

6 The fourth clue is a present and a musical instrument. Listen carefully to a new friend, then play the tune to the end.

7 Do you want to find Emoclew? Here's the first thing you must do. Find a paper to show you the way. Some clever ants can help today.

8 Find the brightest star you can see. Under this star there is a tree. Look under the tree for your final clue. It is something round and blue.

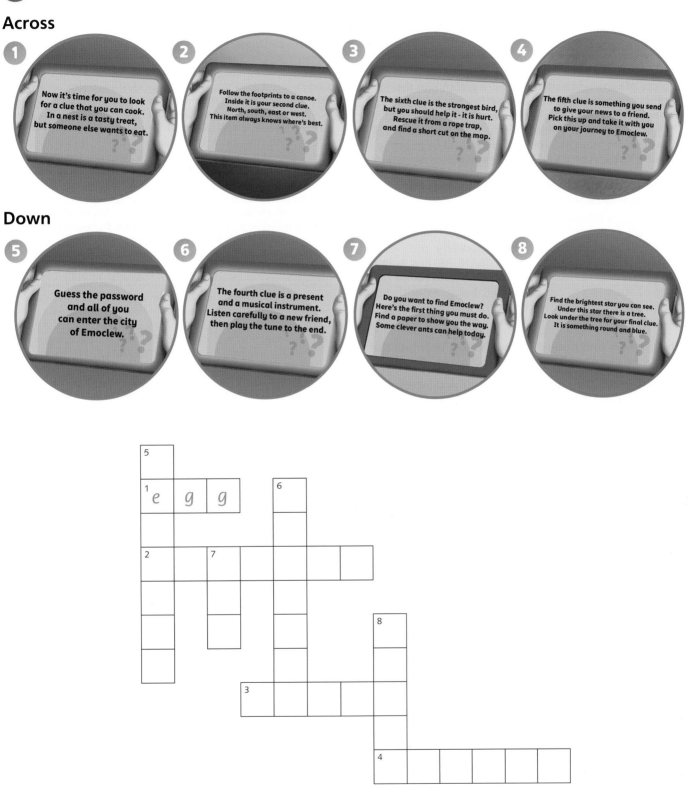

Thanks and Acknowledgements

The authors and publishers would like to thank the following contributors:
Blooberry Design: concept design, book design, page make-up
Vicky Bewick: editing

The authors and publishers acknowledge the following sources of copyright material and are grateful for the permissions granted. While every effort has been made, it has not always been possible to identify the sources of all the material used, or to trace all copyright holders. If any omissions are brought to our notice, we will be happy to include the appropriate acknowledgements on reprinting.

The authors and publishers would like to thank the following illustrators:

Pablo Gallego (Beehive Illustration): pp. 3, 7, 15, 23, 33, 41, 51, 59, 69, 71, 93, 94, 95; Timo Grubing (Beehive Illustration): pp. 50, 70; Mark Duffin: pp. 10, 80; Blooberry: p. 11; Paul Williams (Sylvie Poggio Artists): pp. 16, 18, 49; Ilias Arahovitis (Beehive): pp. 19, 27, 38, 52, 63, 81; Humberto Blanco (Sylvie Poggio Artists): pp. 12, 21, 32, 40, 75; Dusan Pavlic (Beehive): pp. 13, 29, 47, 83; Simon Walmesley: pp. 22, 68; Monkey Feet: pp. 84, 85, 86, 87, 88, 89, 90, 91, 92.

The authors and publishers would like to thank the following for permission to reproduce photographs:

p. 4 (B/G Header): Tim Gainey/Alamy; p. 4 (a): stockfotoart/ Getty Images; p. 4 (b): © Matthew Chattle / Alamy; p. 4 (c): SlobodanMiljevic/Getty Images; p. 4 (d): Darius Pabrinkis/ Shutterstock; p. 4 (e): © Cosmo Condina North America / Alamy; p. 4 (f): celta4/Getty Images; p. 5 (TL): Gustavo Frazao/Shutterstock; p. 5 (TR): John Harper/Getty Images; p. 5 (BL): LifesizeImages/Getty Images; p. 5 (BR): Tier Und Naturfotografie J und C Sohns; p. 6: © Corbis Super RF / Alamy; p. 7: Hero Images/Getty Images; p. 8: arfo/Getty Images; p. 10 (B/G Header: Farianna/Shutterstock; p. 12 (B/G Header): Mister Jo/Getty; p. 14 (Diego & Anna): Jupiterimages/ Getty Images; p. 14 (Sam & Ellie): Shelly Perry/Getty Images; p. 14 (Ben & Joe): © KidStock/Blend Images/Corbis; p. 14 (Hae & Akoi): RedChopsticks/Getty Images; p. 14 (Harry & Olivia): Rosemarie Gearhart/Getty Images; p. 14 (Elena & Leila): John Fedele/Getty Images; p. 15: Pavel L Photo and Video/Shutterstock; p. 18 (B/G Header): Stefan Mokrzecki/Getty; p. 20 (B/G Header): VALENTINA PETROVA/Getty; p. 20 (a): timnewman/Getty Images; p. 20 (b): Graeme Dawes/Shutterstock; p. 20 (c): SP-Photo/Shutterstock; p. 20 (d): © Patti McConville / Alamy; p. 20 (e): Umierov Nariman/ Shutterstock; p. 20 (f): didesign021/Shutterstock; Fabrice LEROUGE/Getty Images; p. 24: Peathegee Inc/Getty Images; p. 26 (B/G Header): Sportstock/Shutterstock; p. 26 (1): Tetra Images – PT Images/Getty Images; p. 26 (2): Echo/Getty Images; p. 26 (3): pamspix/Getty Images; p. 26 (4): Denis Kuvaev/Shutterstock; p. 26 (5): Homsa/Shutterstock; p. 26 (6): ARENA Creative/Shutterstock; p. 30 (B/G Header): hxdyl/Getty; p. 30 (TL/a): firatgocmen/Getty Images; p. 30 (TL/b): Image By Marc Gutierrez/Getty Images; p. 30 (TL/c): poplasen/Getty Images; p. 30 (TR/a): utah778/Getty Images; p. 20 (TR/b): satit_srihin/Shutterstock; p. 30 (TR/c): Tobias Titz/Getty Images; p. 30 (BL/a): Andrew Dernie/Getty Images; p. 30 (BL/b): lesapi/Getty Images; p. 30 (BL/c): marilyna/Getty Images; p. 30 (BR/a): SvetlanaK/Getty Images; p. 30 (BR/b): ajt/Getty Images; p. 30 (BR/c): Jack Puccio/Getty Images; p. 31: Alamy Photos; p. 32 (L): Westend61/Getty Images; p. 32 (R): Bartosz Hadyniak/Getty Images; p. 33: Éva Katalin/Getty Images; p. 34 (TR): andresr/Getty Images; p. 34 (a): stocknroll/Getty Images; p. 34 (b): Glow Cuisine/ Getty Images; p. 34 (c): images72 /Shutterstock; p. 34 (d): © Simon Reddy / Alamy; p. 34 €: © PhotoCuisine / Alamy; p. 36 (B/G Header): Westend61 GmbH/Alamy; p. 38 (B/G Header): maxoidos/ Getty; p. 39 (1): Glow Images, Inc/Getty Images; p. 39 (2): © JGI/ Jamie Grill/Blend Images/Corbis; p. 39 (3): Blend Images – KidStock/ Getty Images; p. 39 (4): lend Images – KidStock/Getty Images; p. 39 (5): Simon Potter/Getty Images; p. 41: © Blend Images / Alamy; p. 42: Daisy Daisy/Shutterstock; p. 44 (B/G Header): Bradley Wells/ Getty Images; p. 44 (B/G Header): arturbo/Getty Images; p. 48 (UCL): © Art Directors & TRIP / Alamy; p. 48 (UC/Computer/web site): Cambridge University Press; 48 (UC/web site main photo): Enrico Fianchini/Getty Images; p. 48 (UCR): Alamy Photos; p. 48 (LCL): Guenter Fischer/Getty Images; p. 48 (LC): pictafolio/Getty Images; p, 48 (LCR): Kris Ubach and Quim Roser/Getty Images; p. 51: Stephane Bidouze/Shutterstock; p. 54 (B/G Header): Tuul / hemis.fr/Getty; p. 54 (a): © Heritage Image Partnership Ltd / Alamy; p. 54 (b): DEA PICTURE LIBRARY / Getty Images; p. 54 (c): © Gianni Dagli Orti/Corbis; p. 54 (d): Cambridge University Press; p. 54 (e & f): © Sandro Vannini/Corbis; p. 54 (g): © Heritage Images/Corbis; p. 55: Christine Langer-Pueschel/Shutterstock; p. 56 (B/G Header): Arpad Benedek/Getty; p. 56 (a): Denis Tabler/ Shutterstock; p. 56 (b): Alena Brozova/Shutterstock; p. 56 (c): sl_photo/Shutterstock; p. 56 (d): Jim Barber/Shutterstock; p. 56 (e): Ivan Smuk/Shutterstock; p. 56 (f): © Image Source / Alamy; p. 57: © Radius Images / Alamy; p. 58 (1a): Ivan Bajic/Getty Images; p. 58 (1b): © Arcaid Images / Alamy; p. 58 (2a): Jeffrey Hamilton/ Getty Images; p. 58 (2b): © Werli Francois / Alamy; p. 58 (3a): Hero Images/Getty Images; p. 58 (3b): Valentyna Chukhlyebova/ Shutterstock; p. 58 (4a): © Image Source / Alamy; p. 58 (4b): Bryan Mullennix/Getty Images; p. 58 (5a): Patrick Lane/Getty Images; p. 58 (5b): eurobanks/Shutterstock; p. 59: RL Productions/Getty Images; p. 60 (1): urchello108/Shutterstock; p. 60 (2): beraten/ Shutterstock; p. 60 (3): Luis Carlos Torres/Shutterstock; p. 60 (4): Dave King/Getty Images; p. 60 (5): anaken2012/Shutterstock; p. 62 (B/G Header): Picade LLC /Alamy; p. 62 (a): CREATISTA/ Shutterstock; p. 62 (b): Terry J Alcorn/Getty Images; p. 62 (c): Coffee Lover/Shutterstock; p.62 (d): Fotografiche/Shutterstock; p. 62 €: © Peter Scholey / Alamy; p. 62 (f): Chase Clausen/ Shutterstock; p. 65: © PhotoAlto/Corbis; p. 66 (B/G Header): scibak/Getty; p. 66 (a): © Sebastian Kaulitzki / Alamy; p. 66 (b): ikoNomad/Shutterstock; p. 66 (c): MarcelClemens/Shutterstock; p. 66 (d): 1971yes/Getty Images; p. 66 (e): © Shotshop GmbH / Alamy; p. 66 (f): sdecoret/Shutterstock; p. 69: Blend Images – KidStock; p. 72 (B/G Header): Maciej Sojka/Shutterstock; p. 72 (C): rwarnick/ Getty Images; p. 73 (T): ER Productions/Getty Images; p. 73 (B): scibak/Getty; p. 74 (B/G Header): Nutexzles/Getty; p. 74 (1): Dorling Kindersley/Getty Images; p. 74 (2): Epsicons/Shutterstock; p. 74 (3): aquariagirl1970/Shutterstock; p. 74 (4): skodonnell/Getty Images; p. 76 (1): aslysun/Shutterstock; p. 76 (2): Maremagnum/Getty Images; p. 76 (3): Tetra Images – Jessica Peterson/Getty Images; p. 76 (4): © Kevin Britland / Alamy; p. 76 (5): © Jennie Hart / Alamy; p. 77: Christopher Futcher/Getty Images; p. 78 (L): ET1972/Shutterstock; p. 78 (CL): © Christian Draghici / Alamy; p. 78 (C): Ray Bradshaw/ Getty Images; p. 78 (CR): 12ee12/Getty Images; p. 78 (R): photo75/ Getty Images; p. 80 (B/G Header); p. 80 (L & C): MARTYN F. CHILLMAID/SCIENCE PHOTO LIBRARY; p. 80 (R): Dorling Kindersley/UIG/SCIENCE PHOTO LIBRARY.

Commissioned Photography by Gareth Boden Photography for pages 44 (B), 48 (UC/Computer/web site) and 60 (TR).

Front cover photograph by Jon Arnold/Getty Images